A Note from David Macaulay

Dear reader,

When I was a kid I did not like to read. But if a book had pictures, I would try to read it. The pictures made reading more fun. They helped me understand what the words meant. Words and pictures are still my favorite way to read a story. They are also my favorite way to tell a story–even a story about toilets.

Everybody knows what a toilet is for. And everyone lucky enough to have one knows how to use it–even in the dark. Most toilets are quite simple, but they all have an important job to do. They take away the waste our bodies make. They are also not bad for reading on.

David

Dear parents and teachers,

Readers, like the one you are holding, have long served as the portal through which children can be lured into the world of words. The most successful of these use illustration to soften the hard work of learning to decode text. But children are not only learning verbal literacy, they are learning visual literacy as well. They learn to read pictures, to pick up clues that may help them infer meaning and add depth to the words.

All the topics chosen for the books in this series are nonfiction. Whether they are historical or contemporary, from the natural world or the manmade, the topics reflect things we know children are interested in and curious about. Since these books are intended to stimulate both verbal and visual literacy, each page is balanced and information is conveyed in both art and text.

To support the reader's curiosity, there is a glossary, list of suggested books and other media, and an index in the back of the book.

It is my hope that these books will connect future citizens with their increasingly complex planet in a meaningful and creative way. If I've done my job well, you will enjoy reading and looking, too.

David Macaulay

For activities and reading tips, visit myreadersonline.com.

DAVID MACAULAY STUDIO
An imprint of Roaring Brook Press/
Macmillan Children's Publishing Group

Copyright © 2013 by David Macaulay. All rights reserved.
Printed in China by Toppan Leefung Printing Ltd., Dongguan City,
Guangdong Province
For information, address Macmillan Children's Publishing Group,
175 Fifth Avenue, New York, NY 10010.

Library of Congress Control Number: 2012947300

ISBN 978-1-59643-779-1 (hardcover)
10 9 8 7 6 5 4 3 2 1
ISBN 978-1-59643-780-7 (paperback)
10 9 8 7 6 5 4 3 2 1

First Edition: 2013

mackids.com

This is a Level 4 book
LEXILE AD 740L

DAVID MACAULAY

TOILET
How It Works

with
SHEILA KEENAN

David Macaulay Studio
Macmillan Children's Publishing Group
New York

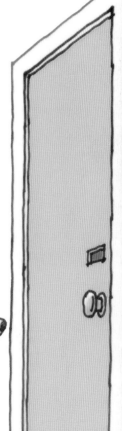

Everybody knows
what a toilet is for.

Slurp. Slurp. Slurp.

Good-bye, old friend.

A spring garden.

A toilet's most important job is to remove
the waste our bodies make.

Tiny creatures called bacteria live
in the waste.
Bacteria produce useful nutrients.
But if they get on our hands or back inside
our bodies, they can make us sick.

With the push of a button
or the press of a handle,
the toilet sends our waste on its way.

Clever toilet.

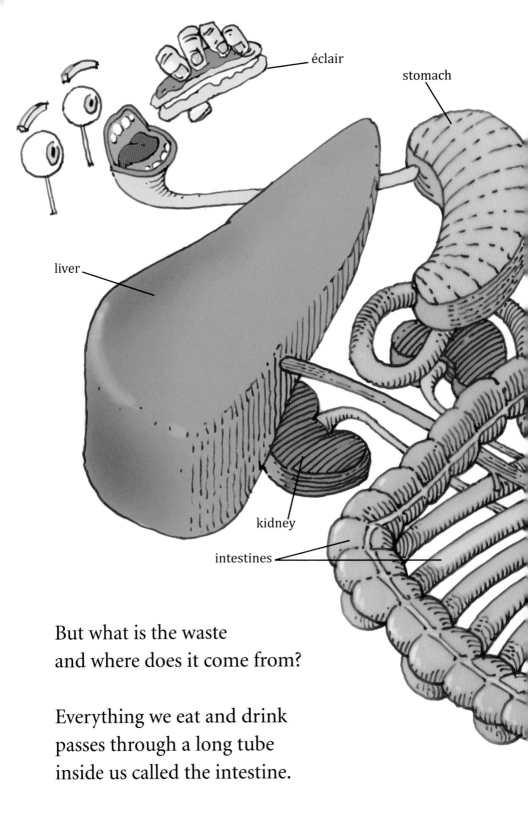

éclair

stomach

liver

kidney

intestines

But what is the waste
and where does it come from?

Everything we eat and drink
passes through a long tube
inside us called the intestine.

Anything useful is absorbed
into the blood vessels and sent
to the liver for processing.
Everything left over is waste.
Solid waste collects
at the end of our intestines.
Liquid waste is processed by the kidneys
and stored in the bladder.

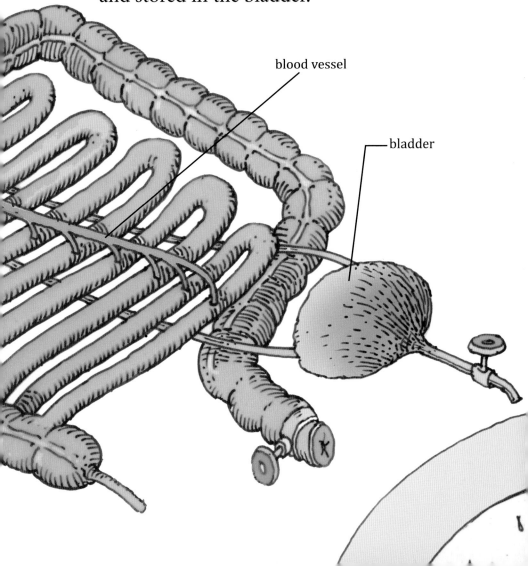

blood vessel

bladder

A few times a day your body
reminds you to get rid of waste.

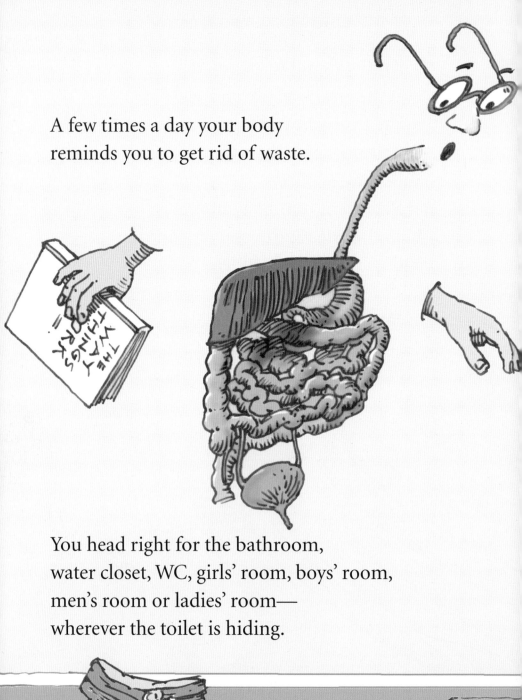

You head right for the bathroom,
water closet, WC, girls' room, boys' room,
men's room or ladies' room—
wherever the toilet is hiding.

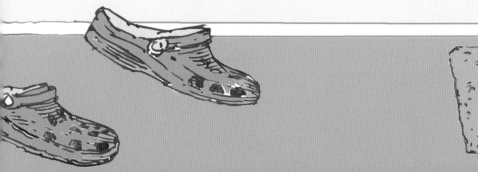

Most toilets have two containers of water.
The one on top with the handle or button
is called the tank.
The part you sit on is called the bowl.
Do not sit on the tank!

bowl

tank

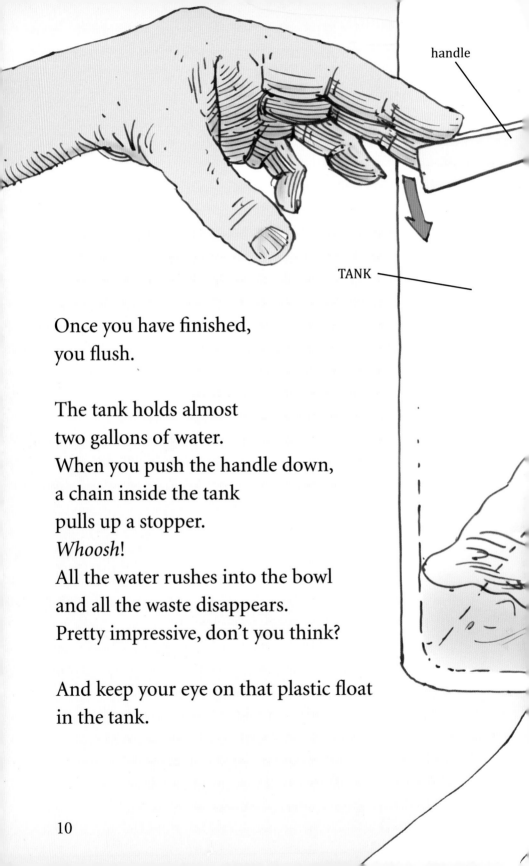

handle

TANK

Once you have finished,
you flush.

The tank holds almost
two gallons of water.
When you push the handle down,
a chain inside the tank
pulls up a stopper.
Whoosh!
All the water rushes into the bowl
and all the waste disappears.
Pretty impressive, don't you think?

And keep your eye on that plastic float
in the tank.

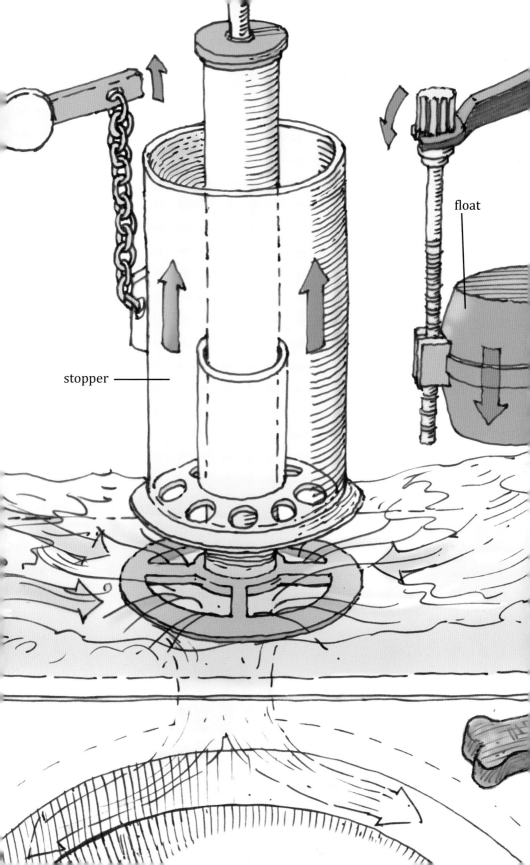

stopper

float

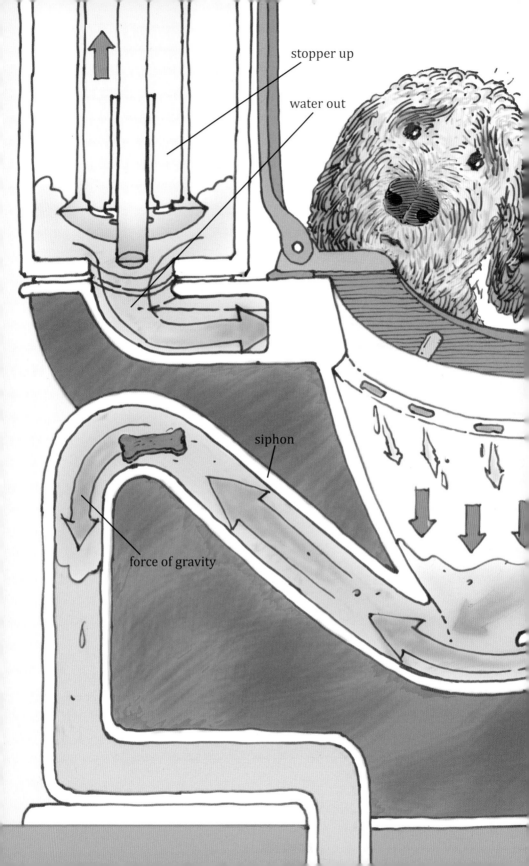

stopper up

water out

siphon

force of gravity

The sudden rush of water from the tank
forces the waste into a specially shaped pipe
at the bottom of the bowl.
This pipe is called a siphon.
It starts with a steep climb.

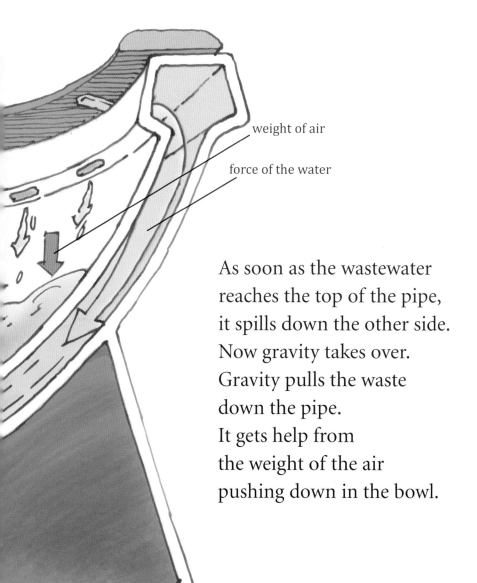

weight of air

force of the water

As soon as the wastewater
reaches the top of the pipe,
it spills down the other side.
Now gravity takes over.
Gravity pulls the waste
down the pipe.
It gets help from
the weight of the air
pushing down in the bowl.

When the tank is empty,
the stopper closes.
It is time for a refill.
As the float pulls down on the lever,
fresh water enters the tank.
Slowly the water rises,
and so does the float.
When the float stops pulling on the lever,
the water shuts off.
The tank is full.
The toilet bowl has filled up, too.

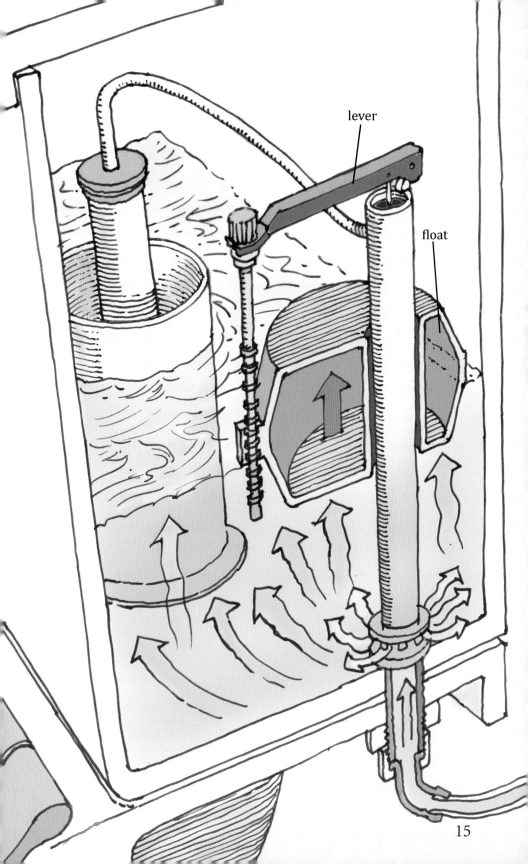

lever

float

soil pipe

All the wastewater from the bathroom, washing machine, kitchen, and hot tub leaves your house through a soil pipe.

If you live where houses are far apart, the pipe may lead to a septic tank buried in the yard.

septic tank ——

As the wastewater enters the septic tank,
it separates into layers.
Oil and grease, called scum,
floats on top of the dirty water.
Heavier stuff sinks to the bottom.
Bacteria continues digesting the waste.

scum

dirty water

heavy waste

You should try the purplish stuff!

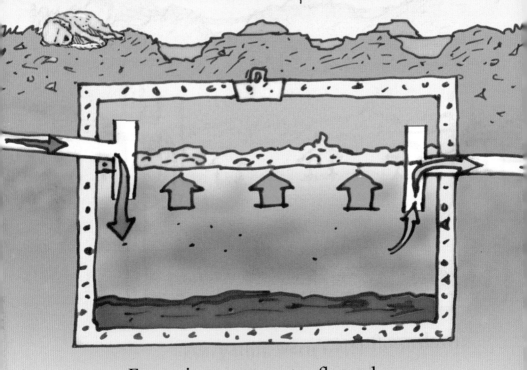

Every time wastewater flows down
and into the septic tank,
it pushes up the water level.
This sends some of the water
out the other side.

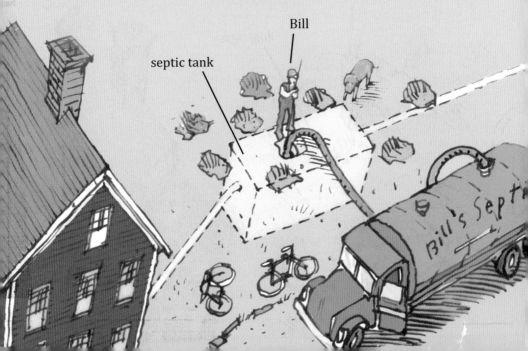

Bill

septic tank

Bill's Sept

Water leaving the tank
seeps into the surrounding soil
through perforated pipes.
This water contains nutrients
produced by the hungry bacteria.
See the happy, green grass?

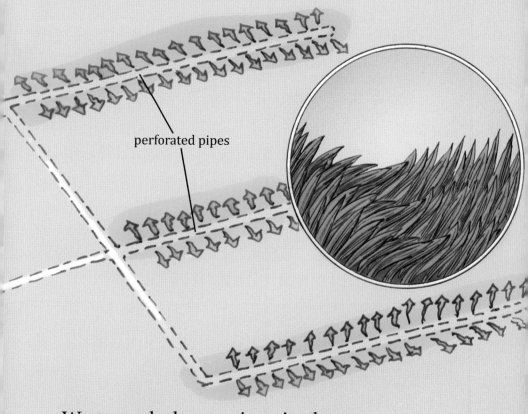

perforated pipes

Waste on the bottom just sits there.
Every few years, somebody has to remove
the dark, smelly gunk from
the bottom of the septic tank.

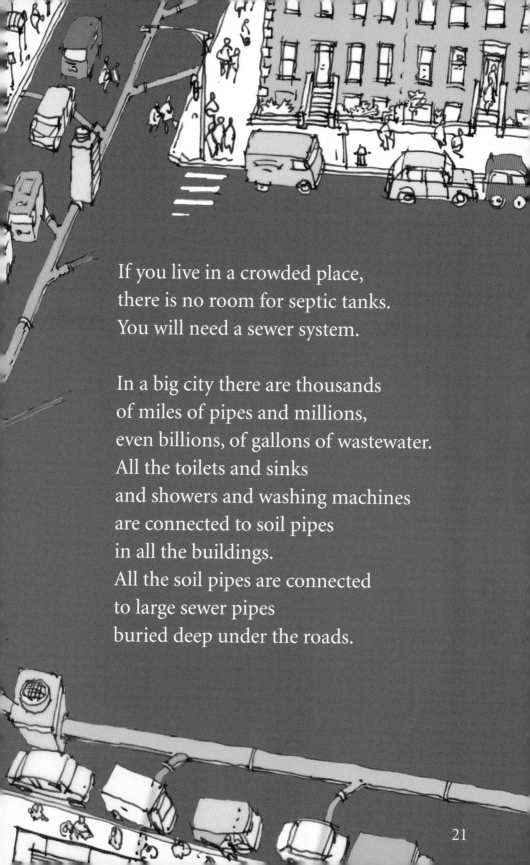

If you live in a crowded place,
there is no room for septic tanks.
You will need a sewer system.

In a big city there are thousands
of miles of pipes and millions,
even billions, of gallons of wastewater.
All the toilets and sinks
and showers and washing machines
are connected to soil pipes
in all the buildings.
All the soil pipes are connected
to large sewer pipes
buried deep under the roads.

The largest sewer pipe leads to
a wastewater treatment plant.
The wastewater flows through
metal screens that capture trash.
Sand and gravel are removed next.

Now the wastewater is pumped into
a big round tank called a clarifier.
Scum is skimmed off the top.

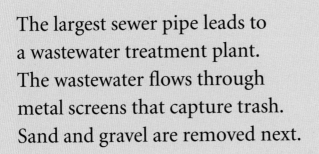

trash

metal screens

wastewater

sand and gravel

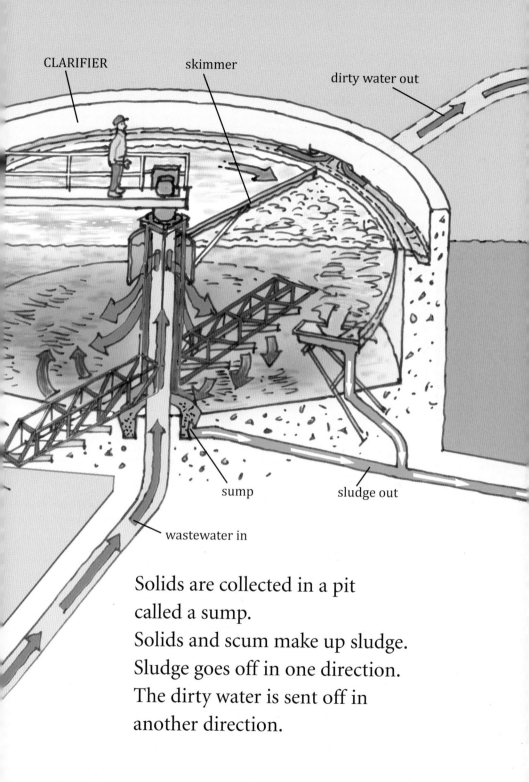

CLARIFIER

skimmer

dirty water out

sump

sludge out

wastewater in

Solids are collected in a pit called a sump.
Solids and scum make up sludge.
Sludge goes off in one direction.
The dirty water is sent off in another direction.

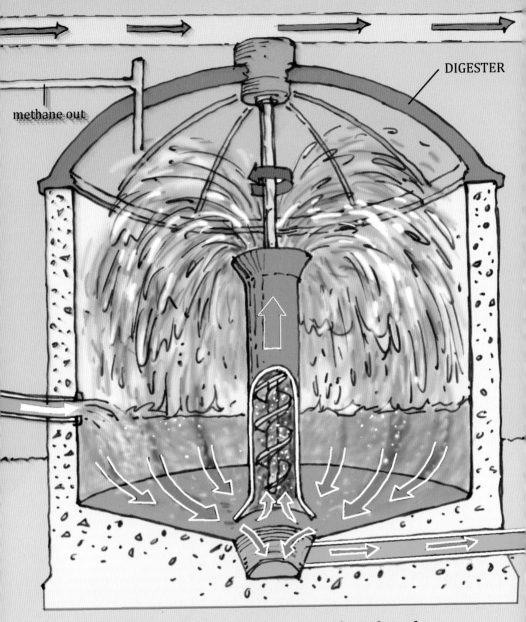

methane out

DIGESTER

Sludge is pumped into an enclosed tank
called a digester.
It is mixed and heated
and mixed some more.
Once again busy bacteria digest the waste
and produce nutrients.

They also produce a gas called methane.
Methane can be used to heat
the treatment plant's buildings or to
generate electricity.

When the digested sludge is ready,
it is piped to a press where
all the water is squeezed out.
This solid is now trucked off
to farms to fertilize soil.

PRESS

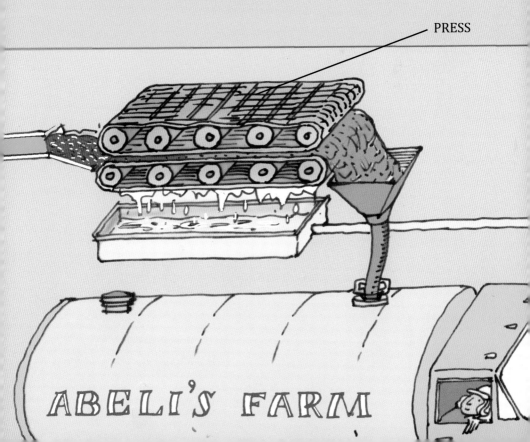

ABELI'S FARM

The dirty water goes into a tank
called an aeration tank.
The water is checked often
to make sure there are enough bacteria.
Oxygen bubbles are added
to help the bacteria.

Then it's off to a second clarifier tank.
Any leftover scum is removed
as clumps of bacteria drop into the sump.

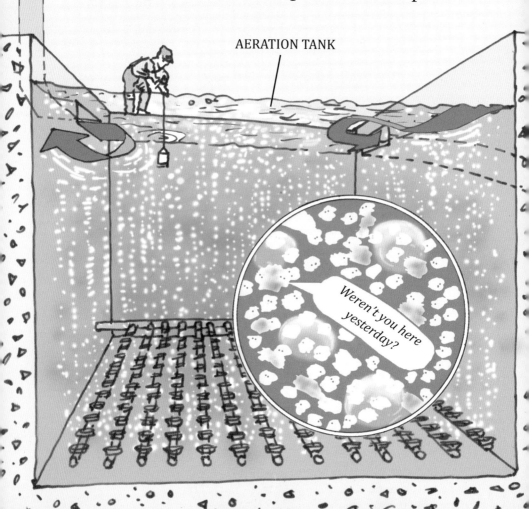

AERATION TANK

Some of these bacteria are returned
to the aeration tank for another meal.
Yum.

The wastewater never stops coming.
So the treatment plant can never
stop working.
Each tank has a twin for backup
—just in case.

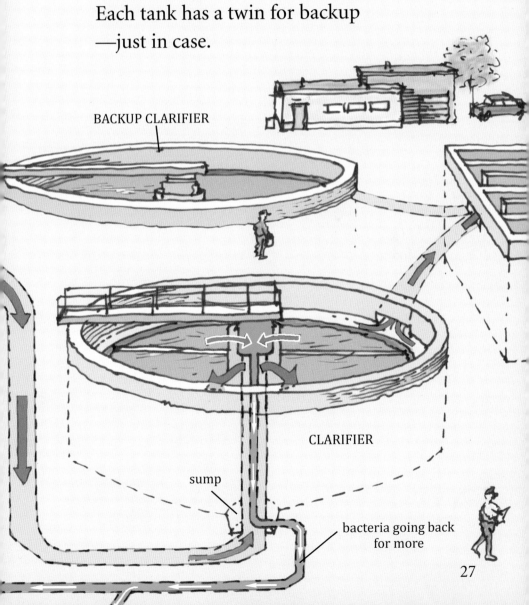

BACKUP CLARIFIER

CLARIFIER

sump

bacteria going back
for more

27

In the last tank, chlorine is added
to the water to kill off
any dangerous bacteria.
Finally, the water is clean enough
to join the river.

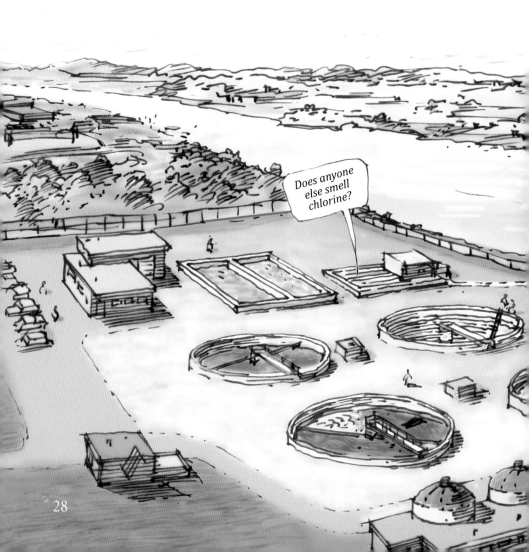

Some of the clean water will evaporate
and form clouds.
Some of these clouds will produce rain.
Some of the rain will end up in reservoirs
as drinking water.

Now you know why we go to all the trouble!

WORDS TO KNOW

aeration to add air

bacteria Microscopic living things that live in us and around us. Some are useful; some cause disease.

bladder the organ where waste liquid is stored before it leaves the body

blood vessels the narrow tubes in your body through which your blood flows

clarify to make something clear

chlorine a gas with a strong smell that is added to water to kill harmful bacteria

gravity the force that pulls things down toward the surface of the earth and keeps them from floating away into space

intestine a long tube extending below the stomach that digests food and absorbs liquids and salts

kidney one of a pair of organs in your body that remove waste matter from your blood and turn it into urine

lever a bar or handle that you use to work or control a machine

liver the organ in the body that cleans the blood

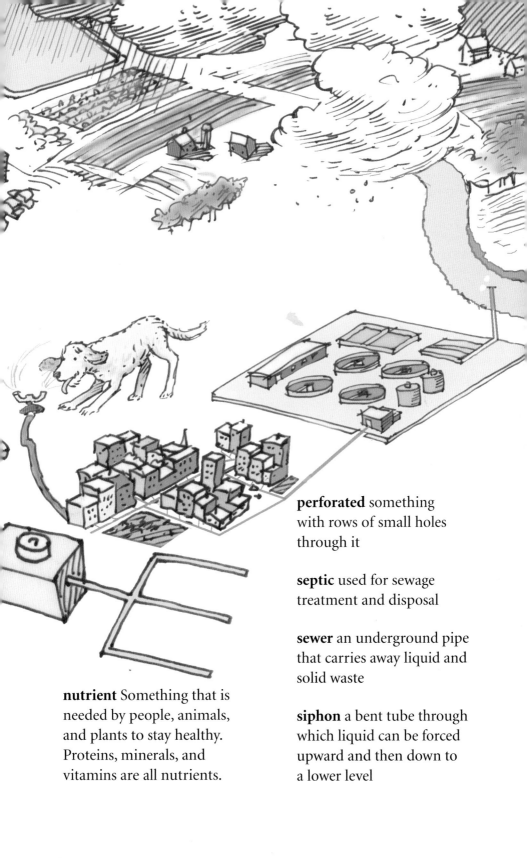

perforated something with rows of small holes through it

septic used for sewage treatment and disposal

sewer an underground pipe that carries away liquid and solid waste

siphon a bent tube through which liquid can be forced upward and then down to a lower level

nutrient Something that is needed by people, animals, and plants to stay healthy. Proteins, minerals, and vitamins are all nutrients.

To Learn More

Flush! The Scoop on Poop Throughout the Ages by Charise Mericle Harper. Little, Brown Young Readers, 2007.

Poop Happened! A History of the World from the Bottom Up by Sarah Albee. Walker Childrens, 2010.

The Story Behind Toilets by Elizabeth Raum. Heinmann Raintree, 2009.

What You Never Knew about Tubs, Toilets, & Showers by Patricia Lauber, illustrated by John Manders. Simon & Schuster Books for Young Readers, 2001.

Sewers (DVD), The History Channel, 2005.

Sewer History
www.sewerhistory.org/index.html

The U.S. Environmental Protection Agency: *Water Sense for Kids*
www.epa.gov/watersense/kids/index.html

Acknowledgments

With special thanks to:

Kate Waters, Susan Bloom, Kevin McLean, David Lord Porter, Katherine Roy, and Ruthie Murray.

Index